Surprise!

You may be reading the wrong way!

It's true: In keeping with the original Japanese comic format, this book reads from right to left—so action, sound effects, and word balloons are completely reversed. This preserves the orientation of the original artwork—plus, it's fun! Check out the diagram shown here to get the hang of things, and then turn to the other side of the book to get started!

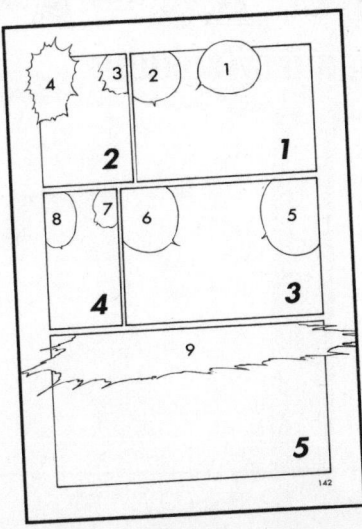

Natsume's BOOK of FRIENDS

STORY and ART by Yuki Midorikawa

Make Some Unusual New Friends

The power to see hidden spirits has always felt like a curse to troubled high schooler Takashi Natsume. But he's about to discover he inherited a lot more than just the Sight from his mysterious grandmother!

Available at your local bookstore or comic store.

Don't Hide What's *Inside*

OTOMEN
by AYA KANNO

Despite his tough jock exterior, Asuka Masamune harbors a secret love for sewing, shojo manga, and all things girly. But when he finds himself drawn to his domestically inept classmate Ryo, his carefully crafted persona is put to the test. Can Asuka ever show his true self to anyone, much less to the girl he's falling for?

Find out in the *Otomen* manga—buy yours today!

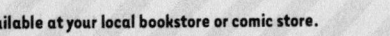

Kamisama Kiss

Story and art by **Julietta Suzuki**

What's a newly fledged godling to do?

Ouran High School
Host Club BOX SET

Story and Art by
Bisco Hatori

Escape to the world of the young, rich and sexy

All 18 volumes in a collector's box with an Ouran High School stationery notepad!

In this screwball romantic comedy, Haruhi, a poor girl at a rich kids' school, is forced to repay an $80,000 debt by working for the school's swankiest, all-male club—as a boy! There she discovers just how wealthy the six members are and how different the rich are from everybody else...

ORESAMA TEACHER
Vol. 19
Shojo Beat Edition

STORY AND ART BY
Izumi Tsubaki

English Translation & Adaptation/JN Productions
Touch-up Art & Lettering/Eric Erbes
Design/Yukiko Whitley
Editor/Pancha Diaz

ORESAMA TEACHER by Izumi Tsubaki © Izumi Tsubaki 2014
All rights reserved. First published in Japan in 2014 by HAKUSENSHA, Inc., Tokyo.
English language translation rights arranged with HAKUSENSHA, Inc., Tokyo.

Printed in the U.S.A.

Published by VIZ Media, LLC
P.O. Box 77010
San Francisco, CA 94107

10 9 8 7 6 5 4 3 2 1
First printing, November 2015

www.viz.com   www.shojobeat.com

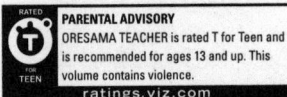

 Did you notice what all the bonus comics in this volume had in common?!

 Huh? The fact that I appeared in most of them?!

 No! Are you blind?! It's glasses! This volume, it's all about wearing glasses! I'm sure it doesn't matter to you, since you don't wear them... But hear me out... The good thing about glasses is... Hey! Don't get fingerprints on the lenses! Nothing annoys us glasses-wearers more than that! You need to stop that if you want to be friends with us.

 Okay, I understand.

 Why are you still touching them?!

Izumi Tsubaki began drawing manga in her first year of high school. She was soon selected to be in the top ten of *Hana to Yume's* HMC (*Hana to Yume* Mangaka Course), and subsequently won *Hana to Yume's* Big Challenge contest. Her debut title, *Chijimete Distance* (Shrink the Distance), ran in 2002 in *Hana to Yume* magazine, issue 17. Her other works include *The Magic Touch* (*Oyayubi kara Romance*) and *Oresama Teacher*, which she is currently working on.

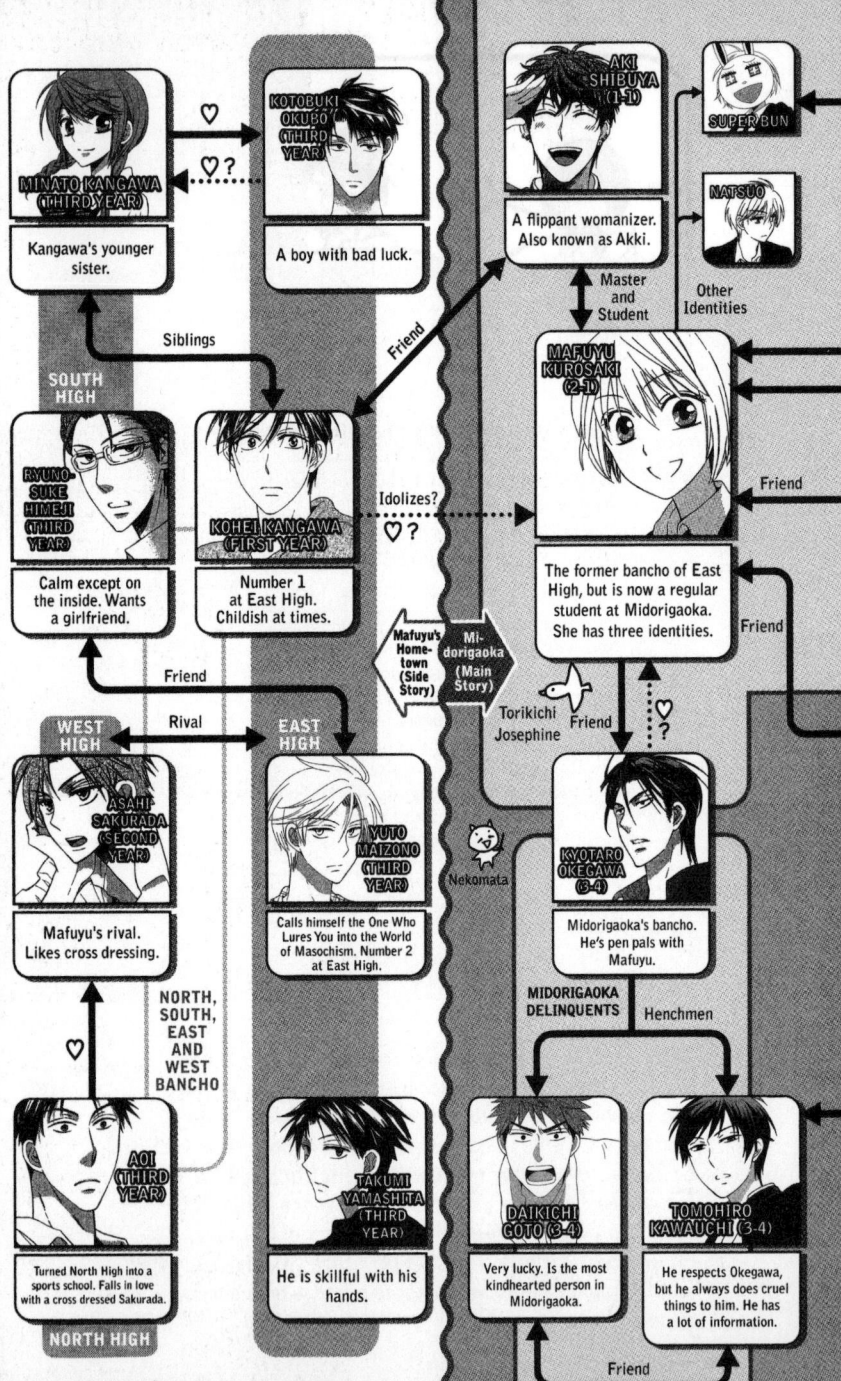

CHARACTER RELATIONSHIPS

A battle between Takaomi and the school director for control of the school.

◆ Midorigaoka used to belong to Takaomi's grandfather. If Takaomi can double the number of students at the school in three years, the school director will give him the rights to run the school.

◆ If Takaomi loses, he'll give up his rights to the land and the director will control the entire school.

HAYASAKA (2-1)

Idolizes

A simple, yet hard-working delinquent who looks up to Super Bun.

Friend and Classmate

Childhood friend

TAKAOMI SAEKI

Friend

The cause of everything. Used to be the boy next door. He is the homeroom teacher of class 2-1 and is the advisor of the Public Morals Club.

PUBLIC MORALS CLUB

SHINOBU YUI (2-2)

Despite vowing his allegiance to Miyabi, he returns to the Public Morals Club. A self-proclaimed ninja.

Crush the Public Morals Club or destroy the school's reputation

Prevent

STUDENT COUNCIL

MIYABI HANABUSA (3-3)

The son of the school director. He is challenging Takaomi for control of the school.

Classmate

REITO AYABE (2-4)

Boy who gets high from cleaning. He is neutral right now.

Classmate

WAKANA HOJO (2-4)

A relatively sensible person. The daughter of an employee of Miyabi's mother.

KANON NONOGUCHI (2-5)

Hates men. Controls Class G.

RUNA MOMOCHI (3-3)

Uses hypnosis. Goals unknown.

Worked together during the school festival

SHUNTARO KOSAKA (2-3)

A human manual.

Classmate

KOMARI YUKIOKA (2-3)

She seduces others with her cute appearance.

Wishes for her happiness

Forgot

KIYAMA HIGH SCHOOL

KENTO NOGAMI

Kiyama's bancho. He has a past with Kanon.

End Notes

Page 22, panel 5: Bancho
The leader of a unit, in this case the head of a gang of delinquents.

Page 107, panel 5: Rokujo Mansion
The home of Genji in *The Tale of Genji*, where he lives with his wife and several concubines.

Page 191, panel 8: Winter Black-saki
Mafuyu is trying to translate her name into English. *Mafuyu* means "midwinter" and *kuro* means "black."

OLD-FASHIONED

EMAIL FRIENDS, HUH?

I THOUGHT YOU WERE GOING TO BECOME EMAIL FRIENDS WITH HIMEJI.

You had a similar tone to your emails.

TORIKICHI HAS TIME OFF DURING SUMMER BREAK

She wasn't there.//

Snow went home too?

A pen pal?!

What era are you from?!

I ALREADY HAVE A PEN PAL.

OH... I DON'T DO IT BY MAIL.

You're old-fashioned, aren't you?

Mafuyu...

I CAN UNDERSTAND...

...THE EXCITEMENT OF SEEING A LETTER IN THE MAILBOX.

FOR REAL, WHAT ERA ARE YOU FROM?!

I DO IT BY PIGEON.

YOU SHOULD HAVE REALIZED

I SEE...

Himeji...

AFTER TALKING WITH HIM, HE SEEMS LIKE A PRETTY INTERESTING GUY.

Huh?

AN EMAIL...

HE'S ABLE TO SAY THINGS THROUGH EMAILS...

...HE HAS DIFFICULTY SAYING OUT LOUD...

BA DA DING♪

Mafuyu ?!

?!

Mafuyu Kuru

Click

Your shirt is inside out, isn't it?

BOTH SIDES OF HIMEJI

Oh...

HIMEJI SAID HE WAS INTERESTED IN MAFUYU.

I introduced him to her.

Email?

WHAT ARE...

...THOSE TWO DOING?

NO.

...

Not at all.

HIMEJI, DO YOU LIKE MAFUYU ?!

Inter-ested ?!

FWIP

Just kidding ♡

I actually fell in love at first sight ♡

AN EMAIL!

GASP

BA DA DING♪

That's right. This will be his true feelings!

IT'S THE SAME!

How unusual!!

Himeji

It's the truth!

She's not my type at all (•▽<) -☆

THEIR COMMON GROUND

THAT'S ...

HUH?

KURO-SAKI...

What? I didn't think they had anything in common...

...MA-FUYU... AND HIMEJI?

...WHO KNOWS MY NUMBER.

ASIDE FROM MY FAMILY MEMBERS, YOU'RE THE EIGHTH PERSON...

YOU'RE THE EIGHTH PERSON *INCLUDING* MY FAMILY.

OH!

MAIZONO'S EMOJI

THAT'S BECAUSE...

...YOUR EMAILS AREN'T CUTE AT ALL.

What's with this tone?

ANNOYED

ANNOYED

WOW, THESE ARE COMPLETELY DIFFERENT FROM THE RESPONSES YOU SEND ME.

WHAT?

Hold on a second.

Really?

IF YOU WANT SOME-THING CUTE, I CAN DO THAT.

TAP TAP TAP

This is Maizono 😊

He can do it...

It's full of emoji.

Oh... Since you've come back 🏠 I've been very happy 😌 But you'll be going away soon 😫 That makes me sad 🐷

BA DA DING

By the way, I bought a 🖤🖤🖤🖤

STOP USING THEM TO CENSOR WORDS.

Want to use it? I would really like it if you tied me up with a 🖤 and 🖤🖤🖤🖤ed and 🖤🖤ed me

MAFUYU'S EMAIL

HIMEJI'S EMAIL

Panel 1 — Mafuyu's Email
Pleased to meet you

♪♪ Once again, I'm Himeji. I've heard many things about you, Mafuyu. ☆ I heard that you're strong enough to break rocks. What are you really like?!

Panel 1 — Himeji's Email
WHAT ?!

THIS IS MY FAULT?

He's pretty weak.

MAFUYU, DON'T MAKE HIMEJI DO ANYTHING RECKLESS.

Panel 2 — Mafuyu's Email

Pleased to meet you

I'm Mafuyu!! This is my first time trying out emoji. I can't really break rocks. I'm just a frail young girl

BADA DING♪

Panel 2 — Himeji's Email

YOU WANT TO BECOME FRIENDS WITH HIMEJI?

YEAH. I do.

WELL, I DON'T KNOW ABOUT THAT...

DO YOU WANT TO KNOW HOW HIMEJI REALLY FEELS?

Panel 3 — Mafuyu's Email

BADA DING

No way!!

I heard you were a bancho so I thought you would be scary! Do you have any favorite foods? I like parfaits ♥

Panel 3 — Himeji's Email

!!!

THIS IS...

BADA DING♪

THEN GIVE HIM YOUR EMAIL.

Panel 4 — Mafuyu's Email

MAFUYU, WHY ARE YOU ONLY USING ONE EMOJI?

...ess meat and potatoes

Meat

is tasty, isn't it?

BADA DING♪

It looks like you eat rabbits.

Panel 4 — Himeji's Email

MAFUYU... THAT'S WHAT YOU'RE FIXATED ON?

Pleased to meet you

♪♪ Once again, I'm Himeji I've heard many thin... about you, Mafuyu ☆

EMOJI!

THOSE ARE EMOJI, RIGHT?!

I've never seen them before!

"YOU GIVE IT A TRY TOO"

Is he ex-pecting some-thing?!

EXCITED

KAPOW

Huh?!

Ugh...

I don't under-stand at all!

Does giving someone a rock have some kind of significance for smart people?

This is for you.

...

My return gift! ♡

TH-THEN YOU CAN HAVE THIS ROCK...

?!

POW

KINDNESS OR MALICE

Well...

HE SAID HE WANTED TO MEET YOU.

WHAT ?!

Really?!

He called me stupid!

HEY, MAIZONO...

WHY DID YOU BRING HIM HERE?!

But does that mean he's trying to pick a fight?

Since he wants to meet me... I guess that means that he isn't trying to make fun of me...

TH THUMP

HUH?

Is it a present ?!

PLOP

KURO-SAKI... THIS IS FOR YOU.

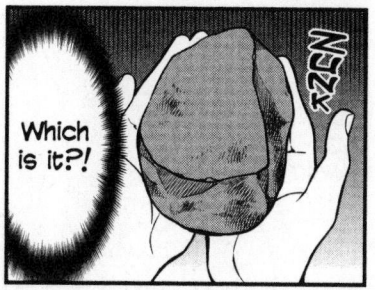

Which is it?!

KZEN

192

MAFUYU KUROSAKI (AGE 16)

ANYWAY, MAFUYU, THIS IS MY BEST FRIEND HIMEJI.

I'M THE STUDENT COUNCIL PRESIDENT.

I'M FROM SOUTH HIGH.

SOUTH HIGH?!

If I'm not mistaken...

South High's student council president...

...he's hailed as their first prodigy since the school's founding...

I need to show him how smart I am so I don't look stupid!

Ugh... He's looking at me with those cold eyes...

ARE YOU STUPID?

*M...

My name is...

Winter Black-saki!!

*IN ENGLISH.

RYUNOSUKE HIMEJI (AGE 18)

YEAH...

?

SHE'S BACK...

MA-FUYU?

HEY, MAIZONO, I'VE HEARD RUMORS THAT MAFUYU KUROSAKI IS BACK.

Mafuyu Kurosaki, the former bancho of East High...

I SEE...

She became the boss even though she's a girl...

I HAVE ABSOLUTELY NO INTEREST IN HER.

Humph.

WHY WOULD I?

BADA BING ♪

DO YOU WANT TO MEET HER?

YOU'RE MORE INTERESTED IN HER THAN I THOUGHT.

I want to see her!!

Do you think she can smash rocks?!

Will she pick a fight with me?! Is she scary?!

I heard she was expelled from school. What did she do?! I really, really want to know!

North South East West

SOUTH EAST ARC

HE DOESN'T HAVE ANY MEMORIES OF THE PAST YEAR...

WHAT ARE YOU TALKING ABOUT?

YOUR MOTHER IS DEAD.

IT'S DANGEROUS TO FORCE HIM TO REMEMBER.

MY MOM IS STILL IN HER ROOM.

THAT FUNERAL WAS...

...IT MIGHT DESTROY HIM...

IF IT...

...HAP-PENS AGAIN...

BRRRRING

PANT PANT

THROB THROB

Mafuyu Kurosaki

...ALL AT ONCE. I FEEL SICK.

THEY CAME BACK...

IF YOU REGAIN **SOME** OF YOUR MEMO-RIES...

...IT'LL BRING BACK **ALL** OF YOUR MEMO-RIES...

I'M...

YOU LOOK TERRIBLE.

...GOING BACK TO MY MOM.

EVEN IF I CRIED OUT LOUD...

...YOU CAN TELL WHO YOU ARE...

...I CAN TELL. *Like your head shape.*

WHEN I'M NEXT TO YOU...

...YOU WERE GOOD AT FIGHTING. *But I was shocked you were a bancho.*

I KNEW THAT...

I have taken something important that belongs to you. If you want it back, then turn in your letter of resignation.

Mr. Hayasaka

THERE'S A POSSIBIL-ITY...

...THAT HE WAS TRYING NOT TO SEE IT.

WHEN...

...

...DID THAT START HAPPEN-ING?

THE FIRST THING HE OBVIOUSLY AVOIDED SEEING...

I decided I wanted to remember.

What was that just now?

OH...

TH THUMP

I need to take a closer look at it.

I can't...

TH THUMP

I'M SURE THAT YOU WON'T REMEMBER.

MAYBE YOU FORGOT IT...

TH THUMP

BUT EVEN SO...

...look away.

TH THUMP

Forget what?

...BECAUSE YOU WANTED TO.

TH THUMP

Who the hell are you?

TH THUMP

I KNOW THAT.

SUMMER BREAK...

SPRING BREAK...

BACK TO SCHOOL...

LAST DAY OF SCHOOL...

CLICK *CLICK* *CLICK* *CLICK*

Let's hang out together tomorrow, Hayasaka.

Oh, Mr. Saeki said to bring your swimsuit tomorrow.

...where are you right now?

...my close friends...

THEY REALLY ARE...

Hayasaka... Please contact me.

CLICK

📶 Email

🕐 From Mafuyu Kurosaki

📧 Sb

I'm waiting in the storehouse next to the central courtyard

Then that story I thought was fake...

CLICK

AND THEN...

HUH?

WHERE HAVE I HEARD THAT BEFORE?

Chapter 110

I made all kinds of excuses.

SNAP

SLISH

CLEAR

There are a lot of ways to see if it's true.

That's right.

I tried not to think about it...

I tried not to look at it...

I GET THE FEELING THIS HAS HAPPENED BEFORE...

HUH?

But...

That's...

...probably a good thing...

I can't remember.

CLEAR

PWR

BEEP

HEY...

IS THIS REALLY ALL RIGHT?

WITHOUT YOUR GLASSES, YOU DON'T LOOK LIKE A TEACHER...

...MR. SAEKI.

ANYWAY, HAYA-SAKA...

We need to find them.

IF YOU WERE ATTACKED IN THE HOUSE THEN SOMEONE HERE MUST HAVE DONE IT.

HUH?

It's no big deal.

NO... THAT'S ALL RIGHT.

SORRY FOR HOGGING YOUR BED.

HAVE YOU EVER...

...LOST YOUR MEMORY BEFORE?

...

NEVER MIND.

NO...

OH...
GOOD MORNING...
...MR. SAEKI.
YOU HAVE A DIFFERENT AIR ABOUT YOU WITHOUT YOUR GLASSES.
Ha ha...
I GET THAT A LOT.
ANYWAY, I HEAR IT'S GOING TO RAIN AGAIN TODAY.
THE MOUNTAIN ROADS MIGHT STILL BE DANGEROUS.
Oh.
IF YOU LIKE...
...YOU CAN STAY OVER ANOTHER NIGHT.
THANK YOU. THAT'S A BIG HELP.
BUT...
...THAT MEANS THAT...
...TONIGHT, I MIGHT...
...GET ATTACKED BY YOU.
...

UMM...

I THINK IT WAS AROUND HERE...

OH.

I WAS MOVED QUITE A DISTANCE.

THERE'S NO BLOOD.

HUH?

RIGHT!

Are you okay?

WHEN WE WERE CARRYING YOU, WE FOUND SOME BLOOD.

Oh, he's hurt.

?

THERE'S EVEN SOME BLOOD ON HIS PJS...

Oh, there's some on his shoulder too.

WHAT?

REALLY?

It was there yesterday.

Yeah.

HMM?

REALLY?

We can look at it later.

WHERE DID THE BLOOD COME FROM?

TAKAOMI?

KA CHAK

I didn't dream of any- thing.

TWEET TWEET TWEET TWEET TWEET TWEET TWEET TWEET TWEET TWEET

I'M NOT IN LOVE WITH MY MOM!

WHAT KIND OF REAC-TION IS THAT?!

Is this what I think it is? Something out of a soap opera?!

...IT'LL REFLECT BADLY ON MY MOM.

BECAUSE IF I DO ANYTHING CARELESS...

WHY DO YOU PUT ON THAT ACT ANYWAY?

Well... Umm..

Don't look away from me!

You're a delinquent, aren't you?

FWIP

!!

YOUR MOM...

WAIT A SECOND! DOES THAT MEAN...

... **YOU'RE MIXED RACE ?!**

WHAT IS YOUR MOM LIKE?

HUH?

IS IT OKAY TO ASK HIM?

WHAT ?!

NO ONE TOLD YOU?!

YOU MUST HAVE ALREADY HEARD ABOUT HER FROM THE OTHERS.

SHE'S A BLOND AMERICAN WHOSE FIRST LANGUAGE IS ENGLISH.

STARE

...

WHAT IS IT?

?

SORRY FOR BOTHERING YOU SO LATE.

OKAY.

WE SHOULD LET HIM REST HERE FOR TONIGHT, JUST IN CASE...

HE SHOULD SLEEP IN HIS ROOM...

He worried us...

IS THAT ALL?

SLUMP

CHAK

WELL...

THIS IS THE FIRST TIME I'VE HEARD YOU SO WORKED UP. "THIS IS BAD! COME QUICKLY!"

You were frantic.

AAAAGH!

WHOA!

THIS IS BAD!

SHUDDER

I can't believe I let it slip!

MY CALM, WELL-MANNERED IMAGE!

YOUR FRIENDS...

...ARE REALLY SPECIAL TO YOU.

Good night.

WHO KNOWS?

—The mountain roads are pretty dangerous.

IF IT RAINS TOMORROW, CAN WE STAY ANOTHER DAY?

OH!

Well, let's go.

I WAS WONDERING WHEN THE RAIN WOULD STOP.

OH...

AS YOUR HOMEROOM TEACHER, HE'S MAKING A HOME VISIT.

WELL...

BY THE WAY...

WHAT DID THAT TEACHER WANT TO TALK ABOUT?

WHAT ARE YOU DOING?!

W...

HUH?

MAKING THINGS UP AGAIN?

YOU DON'T HAVE TO DO THAT.

JEEZ...

Humph!

WHAT WILL IT TAKE FOR YOU TO BELIEVE ME?

...I'd be really happy.

IT'S NOT LIKE THAT.

I'm sure of it.

If her words were true...

SIGH...

Oh!

Yeah, yeah...

WAIT A SEC!

ONCE YOU'RE DONE WITH THAT, WE'RE HEADING BACK.

SLUUUURP

...

Why...

HAYA-SAKA?

I...

...have I disbelieved her stories...

AT THAT MOMENT

...is probably...

I DON'T THINK ANY OF IT IS TRUE.

?

WHAT'S WRONG? YOU WERE ZONING OUT.

HUH?

Like how I experienced the bamboo so I how can he break a wall?

...YOU'RE MAKING SOME OF IT UP, RIGHT?

...from the beginning?

HA HA HA HA!

...

I'LL BET...

I'M AWAKE!

...KNOW THAT...

SHUT UP!

SLAM

I'M THIRSTY. CAN I OPEN THE FRIDGE?

Everyone's asleep.

KLINK

IT'S NOT EVEN SOME-THING ABOUT ME?!

You've got to be kidding me!

PHEW...

AND...

...THERE'S SOMETHING WRONG WITH YOUR KNOCKING!

"IS SOMEONE IN THERE?"

I CAN'T RESPOND IF I'M ASLEEP!

YOU THINK THIS IS A BATH-ROOM?!

Why does it make such a deep noise?!

You think this is a stall?!

...

HAYA-SAKA...

Oh!

W-wait... Calm down... She came here at this hour, so it might be something urgent...

DADDY!
Waah..
Waah...
WAAAAAH!
AAAH!
I'M GOING BACK TO MY MOM.
FWIP
SPLASH
SPLASH
KAORI!
BLINK
SHUP
HUH?
I was asleep...
I WAS DREAMING ABOUT SOME-THING...
...
TH THUMP
TH THUMP

THE PERSON WHO TORMENTED MY MOM IS GONE.

THAT WOMAN...

...DIED, DIDN'T SHE?

IT'S A STRANGE FEELING.

FUNERAL

→RECEPTION

FUNERAL HAYASAKA

YOU...

...

KAORI... YOU...

Waah...

...LOOK TERRIBLE.

...BUT I DO.

SHE DOESN'T HAVE ANY BOYS...

BUT...

...HE LOVES SOMEONE ELSE MORE THAN ME.

...I'M NOT SURE.

HOW IRONIC.

FUNERAL HAYASAKA

KSSSH

NO WAIT!

MORE IMPORTANTLY, WHAT HAPPENED TO YOUR HAIR?!

I CAME IN MY MOM'S PLACE.

WHY...

...ARE YOU HERE?

KAORI?

...a photo of you.

"LYDIA...

"...WITH KAORI (AGE 5)."

THANK YOU.

THERE YOU GO.

THE BOW ON YOUR SKIRT IS CROOKED.

WHAT IS IT, MOMMY?

KAORI...

Perfect. THERE.

THANK YOU.

...another copy of that photo.

I THOUGHT IT WAS A PHOTO OF HIS FIRST LOVE OR SOME OTHER BITTERSWEET MEMORY...

SLIDE

This is...

Is it possible for him to forget about this...

...even if he carries it with him?

"JULY 6...

"IN THE GARDEN..."

ORESAMA TEACHER

Chapter 109

THAT CERTAINLY SOUNDS UNNATURAL.

Introduce me to them.

HUH?! WHAT THE HELL?!

Where did you go?!

They were high-class.

...HAD TEA WITH TWO BEAUTIFUL GIRLS.

SO...

...BELIEVE WHAT KAORI SAYS.

What does Hajo have to do with this?

WHAT ?!

AAGH!

I'm going to tell Hajo!

ALSO, I STOLE ONE OF THEIR PHOTO ALBUMS.

I wanted to see what was in it.

I might find out something.

ANYWAY, I'M GOING TO INVESTIGATE SOME MORE.

WHAT ARE YOU DOING?!

...

I...

SHOOSH

HE'S GOING TO INVESTIGATE THE BEAUTIFUL GIRLS?

...

TMP TMP TMP

...THAT DESPERATE TO MEET SOMEONE?

IS HE...

I hadn't realized...

...

FWIP

That's something I can't do!

Are they going to ask me to betray Hayasaka and join them?!

Hmm ?!

ARE YOU KAORI'S CLASS-MATE?

I AM HAYASAKA'S BEST FRIEND!

THAT'S RIGHT.

YOU ARE?!

I'LL NEVER JOIN YOUR SIDE.

BUT...

FWIP

WHAT ABOUT THE BATTLE BETWEEN THE TRUE WIFE AND THE CONCUBINE?

UMM...

I NEVER THOUGHT KAORI WOULD BRING A FRIEND HOME...

I'M...

...SO RELIEVED.

GASP

...

I HOPE...

...YOU TWO STAY FRIENDS FOREVER.

OH.

IT SUDDENLY STARTED RAINING...

*S*H*O*O*S*H*

I deepened my friendship with Hayasaka!

...

NINJA! WHERE WERE YOU ALL THIS TIME?

TMP TMP TMP

The weather is so unpredictable in the mountains...

I GUESS NOT...

KURO-SAKI...

HMM?

WELL...

PHOTO? HUH?

HAVE YOU EVER SEEN THE PHOTO THAT HAYASAKA ALWAYS CARRIES WITH HIM?

?

WHAT ABOUT IT?

I MIGHT BE OVER-THINKING THIS...

And even if...

...I believe these stories...

...sound like a distant dream...

WHAT AM I GOING TO DO IF MY MEMORIES COME BACK?

WE WERE TRAPPED. WHAT WERE WE GOING TO DO?

...the difference between dream and reality is going to feel weird.

...when I wake up...

These fun times...

RAIN.

PLIP

OH.

IT DOESN'T MATTER WHERE IT IS RIGHT NOW!

HUH?!

Hurry up and get back to the story!

HEY...

HAYASAKA, WHERE'S YOUR CELL PHONE?

HUH? ACTUALLY, THAT EMAIL...

DO YOU REMEMBER ANYTHING?

THERE ARE FIGHTS ALL THE TIME!

HIGH SCHOOL IS AMAZING.

YEAH! YOU FIND THE STORY INTERESTING?

WELL...

WHAT DID IT SAY?

WHAT IS IT?!

Like how strong the bancho is! How can he break a wall?

...YOU'RE MAKING SOME OF IT UP, RIGHT?

TO BE HONEST...

IT FEELS LIKE LISTENING TO SOME FAIRY TALE ABOUT A DISTANT LAND.

HA HA HA HA!

...

I'LL BET...

CREAK

I NEED TO CLEAN THIS UP...

THANK YOU FOR YOUR TIME.

I'VE CUT MYSELF.

...GET SOME REST.

PLEASE...

CREAK

PLIP PLIP PLIP

CHAK

SIGH

...

HE GOT AWAY...

...

AND MORE INTEREST-INGLY...

GLANCE

ACCORDING TO KAORI...

Last time?

...A REPEAT...

...OF LAST TIME?

...

OH...

!

...HIS HEAD...

...IT MIGHT BE BECAUSE HE HIT...

IS THAT WHAT HE SAID?

Phew...

I HOPE IT'S NOTHING SERIOUS...

KLAK

I THINK...

...I SHOULD TAKE HIM TO THE HOSPITAL.

WHAT'S THE DEAL WITH HIS FATHER?

Though he's completely unfazed when I tell him Hayasaka got into a fight...

I guess he isn't over-protective...

I can't get a read on him...

...BUT I GUESS THAT ISN'T THE CASE...

I THOUGHT HE WASN'T INTERESTED IN HIS SON...

I SEE.

KAORI TAKES HIS CLASSES VERY SERIOUSLY.

NO...

HAS ANYTHING ELSE STRANGE HAPPENED?

SOME OF KAORI'S MEMORIES...

...MIGHT BE MISSING...

THIS IS BAD. I DON'T UNDERSTAND ANYTHING.

OH... THAT'S RIGHT...

WHAT IS IT?

THIS HASN'T BEEN CONFIRMED, BUT...

AND THAT'S HOW HE GOT THOSE INJURIES...

HE GOT INTO A FIGHT IN TOWN...

SO...

I'M TRAPPED!

YOU DON'T SEEM VERY SURPRISED.

...

I'M SORRY HE CAUSED YOU SO MUCH TROUBLE.

HUH?

IT'S VERY EMBARRASSING...

...BUT HE'S BEEN DOING THINGS LIKE THAT SECRETLY SINCE MIDDLE SCHOOL...

No one around him noticed, though...

WELL... OH...

THAT HAYASAKA—

THAT *KAORI* GOT INTO A FIGHT.

OH?

I DON'T WANT TO THINK ABOUT IT, BUT...

...I SENSED SOMEONE OVER THERE...

TAK TAK TAK TAK TAK TAK TAK

This side...

...BUT I CAN'T BELIEVE THEY'RE NOT LIVING IN SEPARATE HOUSES...

I THINK IT'S WEIRD FOR THEM TO LIVE TOGETHER...

Hayasaka

Dad

Sister | Sister | Wife

...is probably where the legitimate daughters live!

Lady urasaki

Hana rusat

mpress kikonom

Akashi Lady

This is really awkward!

MODERN VERSION OF ROKUJO MANSION

BUMP

TMP TMP

WHOA!

OH...

I'M SO SORRY.

EEK!

Special Issue Tale of Genji CLASSICS

WHAT IF HE HAS THREE MORE WIVES?

WHERE DID HAYASAKA AND KUROSAKI GO?

FWIP FWIP

They left me behind...

EXCUSE ME... IS THERE...

CREAK...

OH.

THERE ARE ROOMS HERE TOO.

HMM...

Squik

HMM?

ANOTHER HALLWAY?

I DON'T THINK...

SHFF SHFF SHFF

A...

ANYWAY, DON'T BOTHER ME.

JUST GO TO BED AND GET OUT OF HERE.

CREAK

MAYBE...

...THERE REALLY IS SOMETHING WRONG WITH ME...

THEY SAID I'M MISSING MEMORIES...

RUSTLE

RUSTLE

STOP FOLLOWING ME!

I don't remember anything...

...I'VE EVER TALKED THIS MUCH HERE BEFORE...

...so I don't know what I've forgotten.

...there's...

But...

AND EVEN IF I GO SEARCHING FOR IT, I MIGHT COME UP WITH NOTHING.

I don't know what I've forgotten...

...one odd sensation I've never felt before...

...so I don't know what I should remember...

...NEVER THOUGHT OF YOU AS A FATHER.

I'VE...

KAORI!

!

HAYA-SAKA?!

HE'S...

...OVERLY SENSITIVE...

Oh...

I GUESS THAT MEANS HE'S NEVER FORGIVEN HIS DAD...

Two-timer...

OH!

I'M VERY SORRY FOR THAT UNPLEASANT-NESS.

IS HE ALWAYS LIKE THAT?

...

...

HEY, WAIT UP!

Hayasaka!

TROMP

TROMP

TROMP

Wow...

Wow...

KAORI...

HIS NAME IS KAORI...

ABSORB ABSORB

ABSORB ABSORB

Letting it sink in

I never expected to find it out now!

KAORI...

TH THUMP

Oh!

YES!

WHAT ?!

AND ARE YOU TWO KAORI'S CLASS-MATES?

KAORI!!

KAORI!

This is...

So...

...

One woman isn't enough!

DAD

Heh heh heh...

TWO-TIMER

WELL, WELL...

You really can't judge a book by its cover...

At first glance, he seems completely harmless.

THANK YOU SO MUCH FOR BEING FRIENDS WITH KAORI.

CHAK

All this time...

2-1 Hayasaka

YOU'RE MR. SAEKI, RIGHT?

PLEASED TO MEET YOU.

YES.

I'M SORRY FOR THE TROUBLE MY SON HAS CAUSED.

I AM. YES!

THEN YOU MUST BE...

...I never knew...

...his first name...

I AM...

...KAORI'S FATHER.

Chapter 108

Who
…

!!!

That's it!

...

THAT'S A PRETTY AWFUL SCHOOL.

I GO TO MIDORI-GAOKA?

It's the high school for idiots.

We're class representatives!

MAYBE...

...THINGS AREN'T THAT BAD THERE...

I don't really know...

BUT I WONDER WHY THE CLASS REPRESENTATIVES CAME ALL THIS WAY TO SEE ME.

CREAK

I REMEMBER SEEING IT SOMEWHERE BEFORE...

Was it on TV?

HUH?

...

That rabbit mask was pretty creepy...

BUT...

WELL...

I'M JUST OVER-WHELMED BY EVERYTHING I'VE SEEN HERE.

LET'S SET THAT DRAMA ASIDE FOR NOW.

GLOOM...

...SOUNDS LIKE A SOAP OPERA...

Yeah. YOU'RE RIGHT.

He has a huge garden.

He has a huge house.

...

...

Heavy stuff...

WE NEED TO TALK TO HIM...

WE CAME HERE BECAUSE HAYASAKA WON'T COME BACK TO SCHOOL.

It's so gloomy.

DOOM...

THAT'S RIGHT!

HE'S BEEN ACTING SO COLD LATELY THAT I WAS ENJOYING HIS ATTENTION!

THIS ISN'T THE TIME FOR THAT!

He has amnesia!

THAT'S RIGHT!

I WAS SO EXCITED TO SEE HIM THAT I FORGOT! THIS IS REALLY BAD!

You were showing him that rabbit mask too!

Why are you playing with shuriken, Ninja?!

AAAAAH!

POINK

LOSING HIS MEMORIES

TALK TO HIM...

What?

MIND OF A MIDDLE SCHOOL STUDENT

HIGH SCHOOL LIFE

...

...

...

...

!!!

...HE MENTIONED THAT HE HIT HIS HEAD DURING THE FIGHT...

IF I'M NOT MISTAK-EN...

NOW, SHE LIVES IN THE INNERMOST PART OF THE HOUSE. THE ONLY ONES WHO CAN VISIT HER ARE HER ASSISTANT...

WHEN SHE CAME HERE SHE COLLAPSED FROM THE STRESS.

...AND HID THE YOUNG MASTER SO HE WOULDN'T GET MIXED UP IN FAMILY POLITICS.

THE YOUNG MASTER'S MOTHER RAN AWAY...

...

...AND THE YOUNG MASTER.

EVENTUALLY...

...THE MASTER FOUND THEM.

SHE PASSED AWAY QUITE SOME TIME AGO.

UMM...

WHERE DOES THE WIFE LIVE NOW?

I SEE...

IT'S NOT SO EASILY FORGIVABLE.

BUT...

...EVEN SO...

THAT KIND OF...

HE DOES TALK ABOUT HIS MOTHER.

OH.

THAT'S NOT QUITE TRUE.

...HAYASAKA TELL YOU THAT STUFF?

ONLY HIS MOTHER?

WHAT ABOUT HIS FATHER?

No way.

?

HE ESPECIALLY...

...HATES THE MASTER...

GLANCE

...

THE YOUNG MASTER DOESN'T OPEN UP TO ANYONE IN THE HOUSE.

Aww...

NOPE.

He doesn't talk about himself at all.

...HAD TWO DAUGHTERS...

HIS FATHER'S WIFE...

THE YOUNG MASTER...

WHISPER WHISPER

...

YES?

HUH?

?

FIDGET FIDGET

JUST BETWEEN US...

AND THE MISTRESS HAD A BOY...

...IS ILLEGITIMATE.

TOO STIFF?

Huh?

HE SEEMS RATHER DEPENDABLE...

...BUT HE'S A LITTLE TOO STIFF, ISN'T HE?

HE COMES HOME DURING SUMMER VACATION AND OTHER LONG BREAKS...

OH.

...

He's quite the honor student.

Uh-huh.

HE WAS SUSPENDED FOR GETTING INTO A FIGHT.

HE'S ALWAYS LIKE THAT.

THE YOUNG MASTER?

She was the one who answered!

I got to talk to a high school boy! ♡

!!!

CHATTER CHATTER

Oh!

THERE WAS A CALL THIS AFTERNOON! IT WAS FROM THE BOYS' DORM!

OH!

WHAT...

...DOES ALL THIS MEAN?

WELL...

I DON'T KNOW REALLY KNOW...

DOESN'T...

Do they sneak girls in?!

Are there any juicy scandals?!

WHAT'S IT LIKE LIVING IN A DORM?

...well behaved when he's at home?!

Is Haya-saka...

THE BATHROOM IS THAT WAY.

WELL...

GO HOME ALREADY.

CLAKKA CLAKKA CLAKKA CLAKKA

IS HE A SOFTIE INSIDE?

IS THAT WHAT IT IS?

YOU CAN GET TO THE GARDEN FROM HERE. IF YOU WANT TO TAKE A WALK, PUT ON THOSE SHOES.

...THE TOWELS ON THE RACK.

YOU CAN USE...

...showing us around your house?

Cats sometimes sleep there.

Why are you...

OH.

They're incredibly fast.

Haya-saka...

OH...

Oh...

SORRY.

I CAN SHOW YOU THE WAY...

WE WANTED TO KNOW WHERE WE'D BE STAYING...

GULP

WHERE...

...ARE YOU HEADED?

WAAAAAH!

...

HE WAS SO KIND!

That hurts!

POW

!!!

I'm going to gather information!

That hurt!

GLUB GLUB

!!!

...

I can't breathe!

Our first meeting...

THUD

...

STARE

...I need to be on my guard!

That means...

I KEEP TELLING YOU...

...HE'S LIKE A MIDDLE-SCHOOL KID!

Put those shuriken away!

FWIP

SCRATCH SCRATCH

SO LET ME GET THIS STRAIGHT...

UMM...

Huh?

THE IMPORTANT THING IS, WHO ARE YOU?

SOMETHING LIKE THAT. I MUST HAVE FORGOTTEN WHEN I HIT MY HEAD IN THAT FIGHT. *Two years of memories.*

YOU DON'T REMEMBER ANYTHING ABOUT YOUR TIME IN HIGH SCHOOL?

I CAN FUNCTION JUST FINE WITHOUT THEM.

IT'S NO BIG DEAL...

YOU SEEM...

...ODDLY CALM...

Oh.

THANK YOU FOR SHOWING THEM UP.

I WILL TAKE CARE OF THINGS FROM HERE.

?

Umm...

YOUNG MASTER?

...HAYA-SAKA?

WHAT'S THE MATTER...

Hey...

Why are you talking like that?

It's pretty well done!

I HAD NO IDEA YOU WERE PUTTING TOGETHER A PRACTICAL JOKE LIKE THIS!

IT'S MORE LIKE HE TRANSFORMED HIMSELF INTO AN HONOR STUDENT...

TMP TMP TMP TMP

BOW

Wow...

THE WAY HAYASAKA SENT AWAY THAT MAID...

It's so surreal...

Yes, sir.

EXCUSE ME.

YOU...

...LOOK LIKE YOUR INJURIES ARE ALL BETTER.

WAIT!

THE IMPORTANT THING IS, HAYASAKA, ARE YOU ALL RIGHT?!

WE'VE BEEN WORRIED ABOUT YOU BECAUSE YOU HAVEN'T COME BACK TO SCHOOL...

WORRIED?

CLASS-MATES?

I ONLY HEARD THAT MY TEACHER WAS TO BE VISITING.

Hmm?

HUH?

?

BUT I THOUGHT HE SHUT HIMSELF IN HIS ROOM AND WON'T COME OUT...

HE PROBABLY GOT THAT INJURY...

THE YOUNG MASTER IS A QUIET PERSON, ISN'T HE?

...BY GETTING CAUGHT IN THE MIDDLE OF A FIGHT.

The poor thing...

YES.

THAT'S WHAT HE USUALLY DOES.

TMP

TMP

KA CHAK

YOUNG MASTER?

YOUR TEACHER AND CLASSMATES ARE HERE TO SEE YOU.

What is she talking about?

OH.

HERE WE ARE.

!!!

PERHAPS...

...IT WOULD HAVE BEEN BETTER IF WE HAD COME BY TRAIN...

CARS...

SWIP

Your turn!

Yui!

Don't talk anymore!

groo!

N-...

BOTH OF YOU JUST SHUT UP.

...doth have TROUBLE TRAVERSING mountain paths.

HE'S THE SAME AS USUAL.

HOW IS HAYA-SAKA?

THE MASTER STILL HASN'T COME BACK YET. I'LL SHOW YOU TO THE YOUNG MASTER'S ROOM.

HUH?

The same?

WELL...

TMP

TMP

OUR ES-TEEMED TEACHER DROVE US HERE...

...IN HIS ESTEEMED CAR...

?!

WHISPER

Of course I can.

Takaomi, I've been a ninja for eleven years.

It should be obvious.

Oh.... IT JUST OC-CURRED TO ME...

SNAP

WE'RE PRETTY FAR FROM THE STATION.

DID YOU DRIVE HERE?

YES, WE DID!

What?! I thought that was the highest standard of politeness!

WE...

...hath cometh by car.

Are you a samurai?!

That's wrong! Don't try to sound fancy!

Don't just add "esteemed" to everything!

Umm, uhh... In that case...

SWISH...

ARE YOU...

EXCUSE ME...

EXCUSE US.

WE CAME OUT OF CONCERN FOR HAYASAKA.

WE HAVE COME...

...AS SCHOOL DELEGATES.

We're the class representatives.

YES, MA'AM!

...THE ONES WHO CALLED EARLIER FROM MIDORIGAOKA ACADEMY?

SNAP

?

WHAT SEEMS TO BE THE MATTER?

...

Hey...

You two...

I hope you can speak politely.

THERE WAS A TIME WHEN OUR SCHOOL WAS QUITE A MESS.

I DIDN'T MEAN IT LIKE THAT...

Ha ha ha...

NO...

Ha ha ha ha...

NOTHING.

YOUR STUDENTS ARE SO WELL BEHAVED.

Chapter 107

FAVORABLE X 4

Your necktie is crooked.

FINE.

NEVER MIND THE GLASSES. YOU NEED TO GIVE A FAVORABLE IMPRESSION.

Maybe braids.

YOU'LL LOOK MORE LIKE AN HONOR STUDENT...

...IF YOU TIE BACK YOUR HAIR.

I THINK YOUR SKIRT IS A BIT SHORT.

Don't you have anything longer?

You'll look healthier.

YOU LOOK A BIT PALE, SO WHY DON'T YOU TRY SOME MAKEUP?

FINE.

DON'T DO ANYTHING.

SMART X 4

Here you go.

...SINCE YOU'RE GOING TO HAYASAKA'S AS CLASS REPRESENTATIVES, YOU SHOULD LOOK THE PART.

ANYWAY...

TAKE THIS.

IF YOU'RE A CLASS REPRESENTATIVE, YOU NEED TO LOOK SMART...

I THINK THESE SHOULD HAVE SOME EFFECT.

Take them with you.

I got some for you!

MAFUYU!

WHY DON'T YOU TAKE THIS?

WELL...

SO WHAT DID SHE SAY?

HAYASAKA APPARENTLY DOESN'T WANT TO LEAVE THE HOUSE.

HE DOESN'T?

Jeez...

THE WOMAN ON THE PHONE WAS IN HER TWENTIES.

HAYASAKA'S HOUSE HAS A LOT OF STAFF.

A different person than earlier!

...AND REFUSES TO LEAVE...

HE SHUTS HIMSELF IN HIS ROOM...

ONCE HIS SUSPENSION IS OVER...

It's over.

...

WHY?

KA CHAK

WHAT?!

WOW!

OH, HELLO!

NO, I'M NOT HITTING ON YOU! I'M JUST WORRIED ABOUT HAYASAKA!

YOU HAVE SUCH A CUTE VOICE, LADY.

ARE YOU HAYASAKA'S OLDER SISTER?

Wait, wait...

IS THIS HAYASAKA'S HOUSE?

WHAT? LET'S SHARE EMAIL ADDRESSES.

He can do that with old ladies too?

This guy...

...

I can't believe it.

WHY ARE YOU...

...LOOK-ING AT ME LIKE THAT?

WELL...

BYE, I'LL CALL AGAIN.

KA CHAK

I'VE GOT IT.

RIGHT NOW, HAYASAKA IS...

You're amazing, Akki...

RESIDENT ADVISOR

KA CHAK

...but Hayasaka didn't come back...

OLD LADY?

IT'S NO GOOD.

WHEN I CALL HIS HOUSE, SOME SCARY OLD LADY HANGS UP ON ME.

HIS FOLKS ARE MAD AT HIM AND WON'T LET HIM LEAVE...

I DON'T THINK HE STILL THINKS HE'S SUSPENDED...

WHAT DO YOU THINK YOU'RE DOING?!

HEY!

THEN...

...HOW ABOUT THIS?

Wow... Mr. Setagaya's story about his popularity is more elaborate than when he told it to me.

She's taking notes for him.

Umm...

He's been fluffing it up.

See?

Huh?

She's even taking notes on things she doesn't need to.

Is that necessary?

①	MR. SETAGAYA'S DOG STORY	
	↓	
	↓	
	NO POINT	

She's going to show them to him when he comes back.

②	ABSENT-MINDED STORY
	↓
	↓
	ESPECIALLY NO POINT

She's been very diligent.

Do you have anything to do with...

Umm...

Mumble

Mumble

Mr. Miyabi...

...

...THEY MIGHT...

...NOT BE THERE TO BE FOUND.

I KNOW THAT YOU'RE DEPRESSED...

SHINOBU...

I'M A MEMBER OF THE PUBLIC MORALS CLUB NOW.

I FELT LIKE I NEEDED TO SET BOUND-ARIES.

Just come inside already.

...BUT CAN'T YOU DO THIS SOMEWHERE ELSE?

SNIFFLE...

HE HASN'T ANSWERED HIS PHONE...

...SO I HAVE NO IDEA.

WHAT'S HAPPENED TO HAYA-SAKA...

...SINCE THEN?

He's so cruel.

WHAT'S KUROSAKI BEEN UP TO?

AH...

HEH...

HEH HEH...

HEH HEH HEH...

HE ALSO REQUESTED THAT...

AME A

...HIS MIDDLE NAME BE OMITTED.

I REALLY...

...FEEL SO SORRY...

...FOR HIM.

HAYASAKA...

...NEVER HAD ANYTHING TO DO WITH HER, RIGHT?

Oh...

THANKS...

HOW UNUSUAL FOR YOU...

THE WIND GRABBED THEM.

...TO MAKE SUCH A BLUNDER...

OH MY...

FWISH

SWISH

DO YOU THINK...

...SHE WAS GIVING HIM ADVICE?

...SHE SAID.

...BUT SHE SAID...

...ONE LAST THING...

...SOME- THING ABOUT IT BUGGED ME. SO I KEPT AN EYE ON HER.

BUT...

WHO KNOWS?

"...FEEL SORRY FOR YOU."

"I...

SHE HAD SOME STRANGE HABITS.

ALL SORTS OF PEOPLE.

...BUT SHE GETS REALLY FRIENDLY WITH A PERSON FOR A LITTLE WHILE.

I DON'T KNOW HOW TO DESCRIBE IT EXACTLY...

I...

THE LAST THING SHE SAYS TO THEM IS ALWAYS THE SAME.

I DON'T KNOW IF HE WAS IN LOVE WITH MOMOCHI OR WHAT, BUT HE WOULDN'T SHUT UP ABOUT HER.

BUT THERE WAS ONE REALLY STRANGE INCIDENT.

MOST STUDENTS WHO LEFT WERE EXPELLED BECAUSE THEY GOT INTO FIGHTS.

WHEN KAWAUCHI STARTED HERE, THINGS WERE AT THEIR WORST.

Really?

Yeah, that's right.

THERE WERE FIGHTS ALL OVER CAMPUS.

I WENT UP TO SAY HEY.

HE WAS SITTING WITH A GIRL.

WHY ?!

Out of nowhere.

THEN ONE DAY...

...HE DROPPED OUT OF SCHOOL.

HUH?

THE GIRL GOT UP TO LEAVE...

OH...

I SAW HIM YESTERDAY.

HE DROPPED OUT SO SUDDENLY.

I WAS CONCERNED, SO I DID A LITTLE INVESTIGATING.

I NOTICED HE WAS TALKING LESS...

...AND WHEN HE DID TALK IT WAS ONLY ABOUT MOMOCHI, SO WE CHALKED IT UP TO HIM BEING MADLY IN LOVE WITH HER.

WELL...

Umm...

IS HAYA-SAKA ALL RIGHT?

I WAS...

...LOOKING AT THIS.

OH...

TAP

OH.

HELLO.

I CAN'T BELIEVE HE WAS SUSPENDED...

THE TEACHERS ARE SO CRUEL.

THE LAST TIME I TALKED TO HIM...

...HE WAS SO VERY KIND.

I FEEL...

...SO SORRY FOR HIM.

MOST OF THE STUDENTS GETTING EXPELLED...

...WERE TROUBLEMAKERS WHO GOT CAUGHT FIGHTING...

UNTIL TWO YEARS AGO, YOU'D SEE THEM ALL THE TIME.

A NOTICE OF SUSPENSION.

YEAH...

WAS IT BECAUSE OF FIGHTS?

SAEKI WASN'T AROUND YET.

BUT...

...I DON'T THINK THAT WAS THE ONLY REASON.

IT WAS A WILD TIME.

They've been dwindling though.

HUH?

...BUT THERE WERE SOME REGULAR...

...PUNY GUYS WHO GOT KICKED OUT OF SCHOOL TOO.

PAT

WELL...

?

AT ANY RATE...

WEIRD... WHAT WAS THAT ABOUT?

He's been acting weird, but I never expected this to happen...

I'm going now.

...what happened yesterday...

...

I can't imagine him starting the fight.

...I THINK I'LL STOP PICKING FIGHTS.

YOU KNOW...

A ONE-WEEK SUSPEN-SION...

I wonder...

...SOME-ONE PICKED A FIGHT WITH HIM. WHICH MEANS...

And he fought back.

That's right.

ONE WEEK, HUH?

SNAP

...

BEEP

THE NUMBER YOU HAVE CALLED IS OUT OF RANGE...

SIGH

VROOM...

COUGH

HOME?

PANT
PANT
!

HE'S BEING SENT HOME.

I WANTED TO TALK TO HIM...

...BUT HE WAS SURROUNDED BY TEACHERS...

It was no good.

HE'S GOING TO SPEND HIS SUSPENSION AT HOME.

SOME-ONE CAME TO PICK HIM UP.

WHEN...

DID YOU HEAR WHAT HAPPENED?

KURO-SAKI...

H...

PANT PANT

SCRAMBLE SCRAMBLE

HAYA-SAKA...

VROOM...

SCRAMBLE

!

Chapter 106

IF YOU...

GLUB GLUB...

WHAT?

...AND TIE IT TO SOMETHING THEY'RE AFRAID OF, THEY WON'T WANT TO GO NEAR IT ANYMORE...

...TAKE SOMETHING...

...A TIMID CHILD CHERISHES...

THE POOR THING.

THEY'LL WANT TO AVOID BEING SCARED...

...UNTIL FINALLY, THEY WON'T BE ABLE TO MOVE.

THEY'LL CONTINUE TO DISTANCE THEMSELVES FROM WHAT THEY CHERISH...

I forget all the unpleasant things when I'm fighting?

What was it again?

Oh...

I feel like I'm going to remember something scary, like earlier...

I don't know what these guys are talking about, anyway.

That's fine with me.

I think I'll stop trying to remember.

You seem disappointed.

Why are you looking at me like that?

...what I want to know is...

But...

I'm exhausted now.

Send the others my regards.

...people I know here...
It was the only place where I could relax.
BUMP
Tsk!
HEY!
WATCH WHERE YOU'RE GOING!
WAIT...
HUH?
YOU'RE ...
...HAYA-SAKA.
!
HUH?
YOU'RE RIGHT.
YOUR HAIR ALWAYS STANDS OUT A LOT.
WHAT?
IS HE ONE OF YOUR JUNIORS?
Well...
SOME-THING LIKE THAT.
GRAB

...are all vague...

MAYBE THEY'RE NOT REAL...

...memories together?

My memories...

V R R R...

Kurosaki

I'm with Ninja right now. What part of town are you in?

?

AN EMAIL?

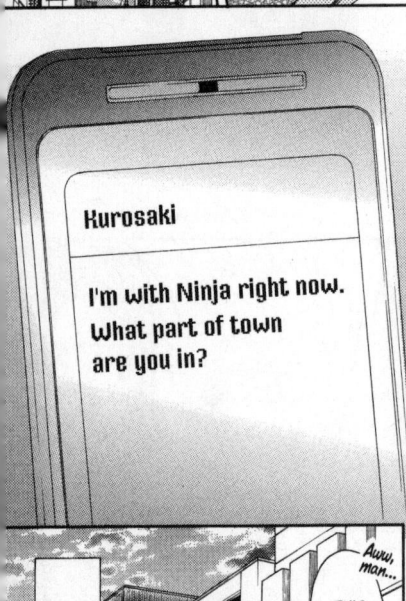

Aww, man...

THIS IS BAD...

THEY FOUND OUT...

I don't run into...

?

YEAH.

HAYA-SAKA?

WAN-DERING AROUND TOWN?

...

...ISN'T HAYASAKA WANDERING AROUND TOWN...

...BECAUSE HE'S INVES-TIGATING?

Quite a few guys have seen him.

I THOUGHT IT WOULD COME BACK EVENTUALLY...

...BUT NONE OF IT HAS...

WHY?

TAK

TAK

SIGH...

TO BE HONEST...

It's been over a year!

NO, HE'S DIFFERENT FROM BACK THEN!

...reminds me of when I first met him.

GLARE

...and irritable...

His defenses are up...

...he's tense...

UHH?

HELLO!

...

It kind of...

YIKES!

TREMBLE

And... And...

WHAT'S A DELINQUENT DOING HERE?

LATELY...

He's changed, hasn't he?

...HAYASAKA HASN'T BEEN IN HIS DORM ROOM...

ABOUT YESTERDAY...

What's this tension?!

...?!

What?!

IS SHE GOING TO CONTINUE OUR TALK FROM YESTERDAY?!

If we talk about the past, she's going to figure out what's going on!

YOU'VE BEEN ACTING WEIRD SINCE YESTERDAY...

W-WHAT'S WRONG?

!!!

GULP

HAYASAKA IS ACTING WEIRD!

TOO LATE

I'll get my memory back eventually.

I need to hide whatever's wrong with me until then...

Things only started to go weird...!!

HA HA HA HA...

...after talking to that guy...

...I COULDN'T REMEMBER ANYTHING...

SKEE

SKEE

IN THE END...

HAYASAKA!

...I should keep quiet so I don't worry anyone.

BUT IT WAS ONLY TEMPORARY...

You're so beautiful!

I STARTED ACTING FUNNY BECAUSE OF HIM BEFORE TOO.

Is it some kind of after-effect?

In that case...

EVEN WITH MY NOTEBOOK...

I need to jot more down!

EVEN WITH MY EMAILS...

This doesn't tell me anything at all!

I need to write longer messages!

Kurosaki

Okay

WHOA!

SHUDDER

MORNING!

I ENROLLED IN SCHOOL...

BUT WHEN I TRY TO THINK BACK—

I'VE BEEN HANGING OUT WITH THEM.

MR. SAEKI

That should be an indisputable fact...

MAFUYU

KUROSAKI

There was a boy always at the girl's side.

The kind the witch liked most...

...the weakest child of all...

He was...

...

WHAT'S GOING ON?

HAYASAKA

...FIGHTING THE PUBLIC MORALS CLUB?

...

WHY ARE YOU...

DOES THAT WORK FOR YOU?

IT'LL ALL BE OVER ONCE I FIGHT THE PUBLIC MORALS CLUB.

I WON'T LAY A FINGER ON ANYONE ELSE.

The boy...

...sent the children out.

The boy was relieved.

The children played with her, and they grew up.

...there was something he hadn't noticed.

But...

He was very worried the witch would realize how fragile the children were.

But there was another kid outside, a girl.

"...come outside."

"...all of the children hiding in the house...

"The rules are simple.

The boy agreed to the terms.

...that the boy had been hiding the weakest children from her.

The witch knew...

"Make...

"How do we decide who wins?"

IT DOESN'T MATTER WHETHER WE WIN OR LOSE AGAINST THE PUBLIC MORALS CLUB...

...RIGHT?

IF YOU DO ANYTHING TO SAVE THEM...

THOSE ARE SOME PRETTY EASY CONDITIONS, COMING FROM YOU.

...I WIN.

IF YOU MANAGE TO REFRAIN FROM DOING ANYTHING...

...YOU WIN.

OH?

Chapter 105

ORESAMA TEACHER

Volume 19
CONTENTS

Chapter 105 --------------------5

Chapter 106 -------------------- 35

Chapter 107 --------------------67

Chapter 108 --------------------97

Chapter 109 -------------------- 127

Chapter 110 -------------------- 157

End Notes ---------------------- 197

▌ Runa Momochi

THIRD YEAR, CLASS THREE. HANABUSA'S CLASSMATE.

▌ Shuntaro Kosaka

HE'S OBSESSED WITH MANUALS. HE DOES NOT HANDLE UNEXPECTED EVENTS WELL.

▌ Miyabi Hanabusa

THE SCHOOL DIRECTOR'S SON AND THE PRESIDENT OF THE STUDENT COUNCIL. HE HAS THE POWER TO ENCHANT ANY WHO MEET HIS GAZE.

▌ Wakana Hojo

SHE HAS A STOIC ATTITUDE AND WATCHES OVER HANABUSA. SHE HAS FEELINGS FOR YUI.

▌ Komari Yukioka

USING HER CUTE LOOKS, SHE CONTROLS PEOPLE AROUND HER WITHOUT SAYING A WORD. INSIDE, SHE'S LIKE A DIRTY OLD MAN.

▌ Kanon Nonoguchi

SHE HATES MEN. HER FAMILY RUNS A DOJO, SO SHE'S STRONG. SHE PLANS TO DESTROY THE PUBLIC MORALS CLUB OUT OF GRATITUDE TOWARDS MIYABI.

▌ Reito Ayabe

HE LOVES CLEANING. HE GETS STRONGER IN DIRTY PLACES. HE IS A STUDENT COUNCIL OFFICER, BUT HE'S ALSO FRIENDS WITH MAFUYU.

Story

★ MAFUYU KUROSAKI WAS ONCE THE BANCHO WHO CONTROLLED ALL OF SAITAMA, BUT WHEN SHE WAS TRANSFERRED TO MIDORIGAOKA ACADEMY, SHE CHANGED COMPLETELY AND BECAME A NORMAL (BUT SPIRITED) HIGH SCHOOL GIRL...OR AT LEAST SHE WAS SUPPOSED TO! TAKAOMI SAEKI, MAFUYU'S CHILDHOOD FRIEND AND HOMEROOM TEACHER, FORCED HER TO JOIN THE PUBLIC MORALS CLUB, THUS MAKING SURE HER LIFE CONTINUED TO BE FAR FROM AVERAGE.

★ THE PUBLIC MORALS CLUB IS UP AGAINST THE STUDENT COUNCIL FOR OWNERSHIP OF MIDORIGAOKA, AND SO FAR THEY'RE WINNING. THEY EVEN HAVE A NEW MEMBER, A FIRST-YEAR STUDENT NAMED SHIBUYA. BUT THEIR CLASH WITH KANON NONOGUCHI TURNS INTO A HUGE RIOT INVOLVING THE INFAMOUS KIYAMA HIGH. LUCKILY, BANCHO OKEGAWA JOINS THE CLUB AND THEY BEAT THE ODDS. THEN, WHILE MAFUYU AND HER FRIENDS ARE ON A SCHOOL TRIP, KOMARI YUKIOKA TARGETS SHIBUYA. BUT HE DISCOVERS HER TRUE NATURE AND THEY REACH A COMPROMISE.

★ SUMMER BREAK! MAFUYU RETURNS TO HER HOMETOWN AND GETS A ROUGH WELCOME FROM HER FORMER MINIONS. THEN TAKAOMI DRAGS THE PUBLIC MORALS CLUB TO THE BEACH. BUT DURING THE FUN, SOMETHING UNUSUAL HAPPENS... THE NEW SEMESTER BEGINS AND HAYASAKA REALIZES THAT HE'S MISSING PARTS OF HIS MEMORY. HE'S DISTURBED WHEN MIYABI TELLS HIM THAT WITHOUT MAFUYU, HE MIGHT HAVE BEEN ASKED TO JOIN THE STUDENT COUNCIL. UNSURE OF WHERE HE BELONGS, HAYASAKA BEGINS TO PANIC...

ORESAMA TEACHER

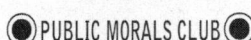

● PUBLIC MORALS CLUB ●

Mafuyu Kurosaki

THE FORMER BANCHO OF SAITAMA EAST HIGH. SHE TRANSFERRED TO MIDORIGAOKA ACADEMY AND JOINED THE PUBLIC MORALS CLUB. SHE ALSO PLAYS THE PARTS OF NATSUO AND SUPER BUN. SHE IS CONCERNED BY THE FACT THAT SHE HAS NO FEMALE FRIENDS.

NATSUO

Same Person

SUPER BUN

Takaomi Saeki

THE ONE RESPONSIBLE FOR TURNING MAFUYU INTO A TERRIFYING PERSON. HE'S NOW MAFUYU'S HOMEROOM TEACHER AND THE ADVISOR OF THE PUBLIC MORALS CLUB.

PUBLIC MORALS CLUB

Shinobu Yui

A FORMER MEMBER OF THE STUDENT COUNCIL AND A SELF-PROCLAIMED NINJA.

Hayasaka

MAFUYU'S CLASSMATE. HE ADMIRES SUPER BUN. HE IS A PLAIN AND SIMPLE DELINQUENT.

Aki Shibuya

A TALKATIVE AND WOMANIZING UNDERCLASSMAN. HIS NICKNAME IS AKKI. HE'S NOT GOOD AT FIGHTING.

Kyotaro Okegawa

THE BANCHO OF MIDORIGAOKA. HE FLUNKED A YEAR, SO HE'S A SUPER SENIOR THIS YEAR. HE JOINED THE PUBLIC MORALS CLUB TO HELP MAFUYU AND HER FRIENDS.

ORESAMA TEACHER

Vol. 19

Story & Art by

Izumi Tsubaki